READING THE BOOK OF LIFE

The Life and Teachings of St Angela of Foligno
for everyone

This book is dedicated to Angela Pickford and to all members of the Franciscan Third Order, of which Angela is one of the great glories.

It is also for the SFO who meet at Ladywell Convent, Godalming, and of whom I have such happy memories.

'Peace and all good' to everyone.

READING THE BOOK OF LIFE

The Life and Teachings of St Angela of Foligno
for everyone

Simplified and illustrated by
Elizabeth Ruth Obbard

New City

First published in 2018
in Great Britain by
New City

© 2018 Elizabeth Ruth Obbard

© Illustrated by Elizabeth Ruth Obbard

Graphic design Sandor Bartus
Copy editor Angela Graham

British Cataloguing-in-Publication Data:
A catalogue record for this book is available from the
British Library

ISBN 978-1-905039-36-4

Typeset in Great Britain by
New City, London

Printed and bound by Books Factory

CONTENTS

INTRODUCTION
One of the great Franciscan women 11
Angela's life 12
Angela's spiritual path 15
Angela's legacy 17

EPISODES FROM THE 'MEMORIAL' (LIFE)
Steps by which Angela advanced 21
The pilgrimage to Assisi 23
Angela returns home 26
An experience of the cross 26
Dialogue about a sign 27
A vision of seeing God as the All Good 29
God's special love for those who have sinned 31
The Blessed Virgin speaks to Angela 32
Parable of the banquet 34
Angela gives an example with the lepers 35
Angela is embraced by the crucified Christ 37
The poverty of the Son of God 39
Angela with Christ in the sepulchre 40
How poverty is the root of all virtues 40
Angela perceives God in darkness 42

Angela chooses the bed that Christ was given
by the Father 43
Angela praises God's judgements 46
With Mary on the feast of Candlemas 47

FROM ANGELA'S 'INSTRUCTIONS' OR TEACHINGS

TEACHINGS ABOUT LOVE
Obtaining good love 49
The properties of love 50
The example of Christ 51
On imperfect and suspect love 52
Perfect love 53

THE BOOK OF LIFE
God's ineffable plan 57
The meaning of Christ's suffering for our salvation 58

ON PRAYER
The supreme necessity of prayer for our holiness 61
Be on guard against false teachers of prayer 62
Effects of living a life of true prayer 64
Three kinds of prayer 64
The example of Jesus and Mary 65

A MEDITATION ON POVERTY
Examples of perfect poverty 69
The example of blessed Francis 70

GRACES RECEIVED IN ASSISI
A vision of the crucified Jesus 73
Angela sees her Franciscan spiritual sons
and daughters 74
A grace at the church of the Portiuncula,
St Mary of the Angels 75
The Blessed Virgin blesses Angela's spiritual
sons and daughters 78
St Francis speaks to Angela 79

ON HUMILITY
A humble heart 81
Love of God and neighbour spring from humility 82
The characteristics of the humble 82
How to acquire humility 84

TRUE LOVE
Three signs of true love 85
On becoming little 85
On tribulations 87

ON THE TRUE KNOWLEDGE OF GOD AND SELF
Coming to know oneself 90

TRANSFORMATION INTO CHRIST
Seven gifts which transform the soul into
Christ Jesus 91
Transformation through prayer 92
Transformation in Christ through the virtues 94

ABOUT THE EUCHARIST
Carrying Christ 97

PERSONAL GRACES FROM GOD
A vision on the feast of the Purification 99
A grace during Holy Week.. 100
A vision of the church of the Portiuncula 101
Christ and St Francis come to Angela in her
illness... 102

ANGELA'S DEATH 105

EPILOGUE 107

FOR FURTHER READING 109

Angela mother & teacher

INTRODUCTION

One of the great Franciscan women

In Angela of Foligno (1248-1309) we have a woman who breathes the air of St Francis in his native Umbria. All her mystical experiences are situated in the vicinity of Assisi. She especially loved the Portiuncula, that little chapel in the woods just outside the city where Francis established his Order. Many of her significant visions took place there as she celebrated the liturgy with her friends and followers, both women and men, who formed a small community around her, among whom were many of the friars. In their turn they looked to her as a mother and teacher, someone who, in her own way, embodied the Franciscan ideal when so many were forsaking it and travelling along controversial paths in their interpretation of poverty.

'You are my only true born child,' Francis says to Angela in one of her revelations as she lies on her sick bed. Thus it is only fitting that she should appear in the white veil of a Franciscan Tertiary among the first and most important Franciscans commemorated in the inner arch of that little chapel of the Portiuncula, cradle of the Order, and now enclosed as a jewel in the setting of a great basilica which Angela had foreseen would one day be erected around it.

With St Clare and St Agnes of Assisi, St Elizabeth of Hungary, St Margaret of Cortona, Blessed Angelina of

Marsciano, and many more, Angela joins that select group of women who, around the time of Francis and later, opened up ways for women to be Franciscan and put their own stamp on the Order as it began to expand; doing this either as individuals or in small communities serving local needs.

And the Franciscan family tree has continued to put out new branches from the thirteenth century down to our own day; among the more recent additions being the Bethany Franciscans, the Capuchin Sisters of Nazareth, the Franciscans of the Renewal, the Third Order Regular Sisters of Steubenville, and many others who have brought Franciscan women into the twenty first century, often in conjunction with Franciscan friars and lay associates.

Angela's life

Who was Angela and what can such a woman say to us today? Perhaps we should start with her early years about which very little is known. She was probably born in 1248, twenty-five years after the death of St Francis, in Foligno, a town near Assisi, and one visited by Francis himself. St Clare was still alive at the time, and her community of Poor Ladies was living the Franciscan ideal in the enclosure of San Damiano. But Angela would not join these nuns. All her life she remained a lay woman, living out her Franciscan vocation as a Tertiary in the midst of the world. Like Catherine of Siena, the Dominican Doctor of the Church who also remained a lay woman, the Mendicant

Orders offered women various ways of being incorporated into their spiritual patrimony.

It seems that Angela's early life was one she would later term 'sinful'. She enjoyed fine clothes and food. She was of gentle birth, rich, proud, beautiful, married and the mother of several children. Everything life could offer a woman of her station was hers for the taking. But at the age of thirty-seven Angela experienced a radical conversion which matured progressively over many years. It began an era which saw her living through a very painful process as she entered on the path of penitence and new life in Christ.

Within a short time Angela's husband, her children and mother all died (presumably of the plague) and she was free to pursue her calling. She wondered whether, with her worldly background, God would accept her. How could she be part of an Order that had already nurtured so many saints and blesseds? Angela struggled on, feeling that Francis was her spiritual guide and that she could find nourishment in Franciscan teaching and ideals without having to join the Poor Ladies of St Clare.

Nevertheless, Angela was acutely aware of her sinful past. Who would release her from the guilt she continually carried in her heart despite knowing she had been forgiven in Confession? With Christ the new love of her life, all the superficialities of her previous existence faded away and, stripping herself of her clothing, she offered herself naked to follow the naked Christ – poor, despised and humble.

The real turning point came after Angela had made a pilgrimage to Rome to ask for the grace of being truly poor.

Then she set out for Assisi, a pilgrimage made with the intention of asking that she might keep well the Franciscan Tertiary Rule she had recently professed. She and a few companions were walking towards Assisi and its newly built church erected in honour of St Francis; there she intended to confirm her self-offering. As she walked up the valley, the great new basilica shining on the hill before her, she came to the crossroads leading to the town. It was there that Angela encountered the presence of the Holy Spirit who spoke in the depths of her heart, assuring her that she was loved more than any other woman in the valley of Spoleto. It was this encounter – the knowledge that she was supremely loved, that she was accepted and forgiven – which enabled Angela to follow her specific vocation with new confidence. Knowing herself loved, her only desire now was to give love in return for love. Yes, Angela was a great penitent, and she had joined the Franciscan Third Order, known as the Order of Penance, but without love penance was not enough. In Christ she discovered a love that had suffered the pains of the Passion and invited her to share in it.

Angela adopted a lifestyle that enabled her to wear a form of Franciscan habit with cord and white veil. She then began to live with a likeminded companion, giving herself over to prayer and works of charity in imitation of Francis, who had especially loved and served lepers and outcasts. This offered her the freedom that life in a religious community would have denied her as a woman, for whom enclosure was enjoined as a matter of course.

Angela is a person who shows the truth that it is never too late. That while there is time God offers mercy and grace as needed. One can be loved uniquely 'more than any others' without having to have led a spotless life.

Angela's spiritual path

Angela, having been a married woman, is never afraid of bodiliness. Her encounters with Christ are unashamedly physical. To her he becomes real, as real as a person can be who walks beside her and teaches her. She sees him as a Living Book. Reading this Living Book is not reading the Scriptures but reading the life of Jesus, particularly in his humiliations, pains and suffering in which Angela desires to share. So often does this desire overflow that we find her shouting and screaming as the pangs of love and participation in the sorrows of Christ take hold of her. We can find something similar in Margery Kempe, who could not contain herself as she wept over the Passion. We are not used to this behaviour in our carefully manicured spiritual lives, but as with Margery, it may be too that Angela carried within herself a sense that only in making a noise would she, as a woman, be heard. And it certainly did not stop her being a full contemplative, given to silence and adoration as much as to physical identification with Christ, her Spouse and Lover.

In sharing her experiences with her confessor, Brother Arnold (her Franciscan uncle who wrote down all that

Angela told him) and with other friars, Angela became a spiritual mother – 'Mother Angela'. It was the friars who were around her as she died, listening for her last words, seeing to her honourable burial and disseminating her teaching after her death.

Angela's life and writings, like those of many women mystics, are being read once more, although she never was completely unknown or forgotten. I myself, who am not a person who usually likes visionaries, cannot help but love Angela. She is so real, so totally 'given' in her love for Christ, so ready to do everything she can to make him known and loved, and so intent on sharing her love for, and understanding of, what it means to be a follower of Francis who gave up all things to follow, naked, the naked Christ.

To go to Assisi, even today, is to breathe the air of simplicity, joy and peace and to revel in the beauty of creation, seeing the same sights today, that both Francis and Angela saw, still relatively unchanged. The little chapel of the Portiuncula, so dear to the hearts of both, still exerts its fascination, despite being enclosed in a great basilica. We can imagine Angela seeing it in its pristine state, a small church in the woods, where once Clare had come from the city at night, running swiftly down into the valley to receive the habit of penance from the hands of Francis himself, and where Francis had asked to die, lying naked on the bare ground – only accepting a patched habit in obedience to his superior.

We who are used to a more sanitised spirituality can find it difficult to resonate with some of Angela's heroic gestures, but we can admire and partake of them in our own small way. Above all, we too can read that Living Book which is Jesus, and be consoled that Angela, who had led a dissipated and 'worldly' life, could reach the heights of sanctity by force of her great desire to hold nothing back from God, come what may.

Angela's legacy

Angela herself did not write, but her words were transcribed by Brother Arnold and translated by him into Latin. They are made up of two parts: the 'Memorial' which focuses on her life and visionary experiences, and the 'Instructions' or teachings, that come from her letters and conferences. She is a woman of the Passion, but she also speaks of the Trinity, the Eucharist, and how we can progress in prayer.

Angela was acclaimed by the people of Foligno and the Church in general as a great and holy woman teacher. She was officially beatified by the Umbrian-born Pope Clement XI in 1701, but canonised by Pope Francis only in 2013. He declared, without need for further miracles or proofs, that she was now a saint whose teaching was such as to be worthy of canonisation without the usual process. (He did the same for Hildegard of Bingen in making her a Doctor of the Church.)

Angela died at the age of sixty-one on January 4th 1309. Her tomb is in the crypt of the Franciscan church of that city.

In this book I rely on the 'Complete Works of Angela of Foligno' in the Classics of Western Spirituality series, translated from the original by Paul Lachance, and also the book of 'The Visions, Revelations and Teachings of Angela of Foligno' selected and modernised by Margaret Galyon. Angela's text ranges from direct speech with Brother Arnold to questions answered, dialogue about various subjects, letters and visionary experiences. I have simplified these, making everything Angela's direct speech as if she were talking directly to the reader. I have also had to choose what to include and what to exclude as she repeats herself in many ways; this is not surprising in that her book is an unedited collection of conversations and writings, transcribed by a 'Brother Scribe' not Angela herself.

May Angela help each of us to go on the pilgrimage of life, like she did, in the assurance that we are loved and chosen 'more than any other in the valley of Spoleto'.

As always, I have had to select and tell in my own words what I think is most important in Angela's book, making use of illustrations to convey the text in an understandable manner.

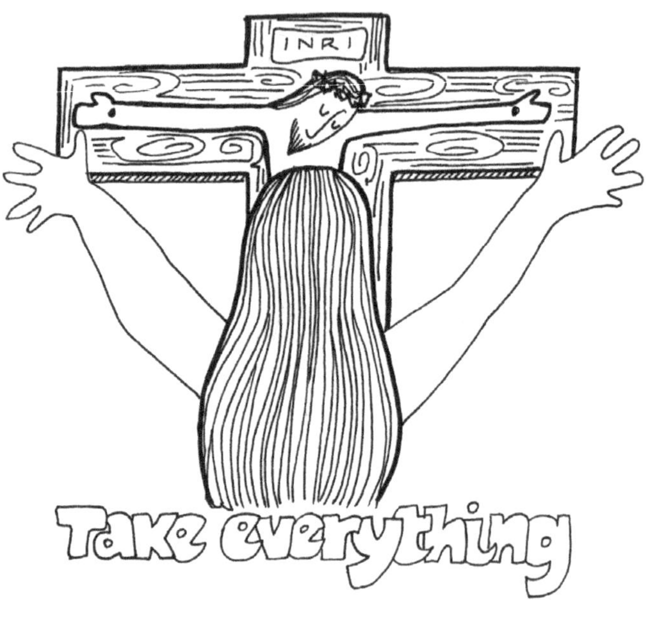
INRI
Take everything

EPISODES FROM THE 'MEMORIAL' (LIFE)

Steps by which Angela advanced

Mine was a long and painful process of purification, some of which I share with you. I do this so that you will understand what kind of person I was before God began to possess my heart.

First I had to realise my sinfulness and confess my sins. In doing this I had no feelings of love, only deep sorrow. In the past I had often been too ashamed to confess fully and had received Communion in a state displeasing to God, but I asked blessed Francis to find me a confessor I could trust and the blessed Francis heard me and granted my request.

I then had to do penance for sin and grow in awareness of the divine mercy and of my own self. As I received more light I wept and grieved over my sinfulness. Spiritual growth takes time. We cannot cut the process short. But gradually I began to look upon the cross and to love the Crucified One who had suffered for me. Stripping myself naked before the crucifix I promised chastity and begged him to keep me faithful.

I also realised that stripping must include detachment from people and possessions. Within a short time all my loved ones were taken from me and so I was free to embrace the cross and become truly poor. From then on I

I LOVE YOU MORE THAN ANY OTHER WOMAN IN THE VALLEY OF SPOLETO
the SPIRIT speaks

began to understand more clearly the love of God and what I must do to respond, cost what it may.

The pilgrimage to Assisi

I had gone to Rome to beg St Peter to obtain for me from God the grace to live in perfect poverty, and I felt that God granted me the grace I asked for. Then I asked blessed Francis to obtain from God for me a feeling of the presence of Christ within me, and grace to observe well the Third Order Rule I had recently professed.

And so I was making my way to the church of St Francis, praying as I walked along. When I reached the crossroads that lie between Spello and Assisi the Holy Sprit addressed me, saying that he had come to accompany me on my journey and give me such consolation as I had never tasted before.

He said, 'You will be able to do nothing but listen to me because I have bound you fast; and I will not leave you until you enter the church of St Francis. Then this particular consolation will leave you, but I will never leave you.'

Then the Spirit began to say to me very tenderly, 'My daughter, my dear and sweet daughter, my delight, my temple, my beloved daughter, love me because you are very much loved by me, much more than you could love me. You are my daughter and my sweet spouse. I love you more than any other woman in this valley of Spoleto.'

I was afraid these words would become a source of vanity but, try as I might, I could not be complacent or vain about them. I looked at the vineyards around me to try and fill my mind with other things but everywhere I looked I could only hear the Spirit saying, 'This is my creation.' and I was filled with sweetness.

After this I was given a vivid remembrance of my sins, but I remained convinced that the Lord and his Mother had spoken to me. To free me from doubt the voice continued, saying, 'I am the one who was crucified for you. I have known hunger and thirst for love of you. I shed my blood for you. I have loved you so much.' And he related to me his entire Passion.

I ENTER INTO YOUR DEEPEST SELF

Feelings come & go but if you love me I will remain

I WILL NEVER LEAVE YOU

I was invited to ask whatever I wanted for myself and my companions but I was sure I was unworthy. The thought of my sinfulness surged back into my memory but the Spirit assured me that if I tried to speak with my companions I would be unable to, for the Lord would fill my thoughts. And in fact the sweetness I experienced was so great I did not even want to reach my destination. All I wanted was to keep on walking, listening, and being loved.

I just cannot describe the sweetness I felt when I heard God saying, 'I am the Holy Spirit who enters into your deepest self.' And he stayed with me, accompanying me as far as St Francis' church.

The second time I went into the church, in the upper basilica, I saw a window depicting Francis being held close to Christ and I heard the Spirit telling me that God would hold me even more closely. Then I was told that though God would withdraw the consolation I felt, he would never leave me as long as I loved him.

Then I saw something full of such immense majesty that I do not know how to describe it, but it seemed to me that it was the All Good. Moreover he spoke words of comfort to me as he withdrew from me very gently and gradually.

At this I began to shout and cry out, 'Love still unknown, why do you leave me?' As I shouted I wanted to die, living was so painful to me. It was during my return to Foligno that I was told that I would experience the cross and the love of God within me and that this would have repercussions even in my body.

Angela returns home

For eight days I still experienced great sweetness. I felt so peaceful just lying down that I was hardly able to rise or do anything, not even say the 'Our Father' and so I longed to die rather than remain in this world.

Then the Spirit said to me at the moment of his departure, 'You are holding the ring of my love. From now on you are engaged to me and you will never leave me. May the blessing of the Father, the Son, and the Holy Spirit be upon you and your companion. Your whole life, your eating and drinking, your sleeping and all that you do are pleasing to me.'

Then my companion heard these words, 'The Holy Spirit is within Lella.'

An experience of the cross

I was pondering on the sufferings Christ endured on the cross, thinking about the nails which, I had heard, had driven a bit of his hands and feet into the wood and I desired to see something of that blessed flesh. So great was my sorrow over the sufferings of Christ that I had to sit down. I stretched my arms on the ground and bent my head on them and Christ showed me his throat and his arms.

Then I was suddenly filled with a joy beyond anything I had ever felt before. Such was Christ's beauty that I knew I was seeing his divinity. I just knew I was in the presence of

God, everything was so clear and bright in the way I sometimes see Christ's body at the elevation of the Host.

Dialogue about a sign

I wanted some kind of sign, a permanent keepsake that would remind me that God had truly spoken to me. I thought I might be given a candle, a precious stone, or something similar, which would remove all doubt and I promised that I would show it to no one else.

God said, 'This sign you are asking for, one which would always give you joy whenever you saw it or touched it, would not take away your doubt. Furthermore, in such a sign you could be deceived. I am about to give you a much better sign which will be continually in the depths of your soul. From it you will always feel something of God's presence and be burning with love for him. And you will recognise in your deep self that no one but I could do such a thing.

'Here, then, is the sign which a place in the depths of your soul, better than what you have asked for. I place in your soul a longing for me so great that your soul will be continually burning for me. So ardent will be this love that if anyone should speak offensively to you you will take it as a grace and cry out that you are unworthy. Know that I myself suffered from such offences with great humility and patience.

'Behold, I now anoint you with a fragrant ointment, one with which a saint, called Saint Syricus, was often anointed, as well as many other saints.' And when I was anointed, I felt great sweetness and a desire for torment and martyrdom.

A vision of seeing God as the All Good

Once I saw a fullness and brightness as if I was in the presence of God and his saints. God said to me, 'I hide some of the great love I have for you.' And I understood that he was showing me very little of his love, virtually nothing in comparison with the reality.

Then I asked him, 'Why do you love me so much? I am such a sinner and have greatly offended you.' God replied, 'Such is the love I have placed in you that I am completely unable to remember your faults. In you I have deposited a great treasure.' And suddenly I realised that this was true. I felt and saw the eyes of God looking at me, and I felt such delight that no saint could come down to earth and express this adequately in words.

God also told me that he was keeping much of his love hidden from me because I would be unable to bear it. When I asked him to give me the strength and grace to bear it I was told that it was good for me to hunger for God

> I HAVE DEPOSITED IN YOU A GREAT treasure
> A LOVE THAT forgives & renews

and not receive all I wanted just for the asking. We need to hunger, to desire, to languish for God rather than be sated. Our need is God's opportunity.

God also told me that there is no excuse for not loving him. Everyone can love God in return for love given. God asks only love for love, and those who really love cannot hold back anything for self. We see this in Jesus who held nothing back. His passion and cross are living proof of his great love.

God's special love for those who have sinned

I was telling God about all my sins, showing him my neediness, and he told me that Mary Magdalene grieved over her sins too, and wanted to be freed from them. Those who have a similar desire to hers can regain their health and wholeness just as she did.

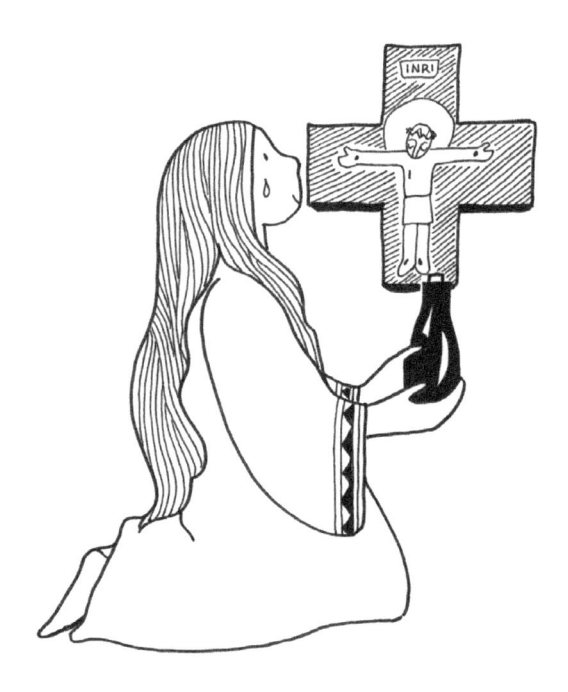

He also told me that those children of his who have sinned greatly, withdrawing from the kingdom and becoming children of the devil rather than children of God, make him greatly rejoice when they return to him. He shows how specially joyful he is by granting them a unique grace that is not granted to virgins and others who have never left him.

In grieving over their fall and sinfulness, people like Mary Magdalene receive a special joy. They know themselves worthy of damnation yet experience the joyful love of the Father on their return. Those who wish to stay in a state of grace after falling should never turn their eyes away from the cross, whether God gives or allows joy or sadness in their lives.

The Blessed Virgin speaks to Angela

One day, as I was present at the elevation of the Host, I heard these words addressed to me by the Blessed Virgin, 'My daughter, sweet to my son and to me, my son has already come to you and blessed you. Now it is fitting that I too come to you and give you my blessing, the blessing of both Mother and son. Work with all your might at loving, for you are greatly loved.'

When the Body of Christ was elevated by the priest I genuflected and adored him and my joy increased. I heard the words of consecration and though other people were kneeling I remained standing. Often I hear my very bones cracking and becoming disjointed, especially my hands, at the time when the Host is elevated.

you are much LOVED

RECEIVE MY BLESSING

WORK HARD AT LOVING

Parable of the banquet

Imagine a man who has a number of friends. He invites them all to a lavish banquet and is grief-stricken when many refuse. Everyone who turns up he seats at his banqueting table. He loves all his guests but some he loves more than others. Those most loved are placed at a table near him and some even get to eat from the same plate and drink from the same cup.

'Tell me, Lord,' I asked, 'When do you send out this invitation?' God then told me that he invites all to eternal life. 'Let everyone come then, for all are called. No one

Come to the banquet

can excuse themselves saying they were not called. And if you want to know how much I love them then look at the cross.'

I wanted to know how those who came arrived at the banquet and I was told that they came by way of suffering and trials; trials that come to those who are virgins, who are chaste, the poor, the long-suffering and the sick. What God was trying to tell me was that my own trials and loss of children and possessions were all sent by God. These things can trouble us at first but then we come to realise that everything comes from God, and so we are able to endure sorrow peacefully.

Angela gives an example with the lepers

Those who are chosen might experience bitterness under trials but we can find sweetness in bitterness as I shall tell.

One Maundy Thursday I suggested to my companion that we find Christ in the hospital among the poor and suffering. We brought with us all the head veils we could carry, and these were sold by a hospital servant so that we could buy food for those in the hospital to eat. Some fish was bought and we added to it all the bread we had to live on.

After this we washed the feet of the women, the hands of the men, and especially those of one of the lepers who had festering sores in an advanced stage of decomposition. Then we drank the water in which we had washed him. And the drink was so sweet that all the way

be merciful • serve with joy

home we tasted its sweetness as if we had received Holy Communion. A small scale of the leper's sores had stuck in my throat. I did not want to spit it out but tried to swallow it just as if I had actually received Communion.

Angela is embraced by the crucified Christ

Once I was gazing at the cross during Vespers. And while I looked with my bodily eyes my soul was suddenly set ablaze with love. I felt every member of my body suffused with joy. For I saw and felt that Christ was within me, embracing my soul with the very arm with which he was crucified. The joy and sense of security this gave me were very great.

This made me understand that we shall see the flesh of Christ and in heaven be made one with him. I was so completely certain that God was at work in me that I could not doubt it.

My present delight is to see the hand he shows me with the nail marks, and to hear him say, 'See what I suffered for you and others.' Truly I cannot be sad concerning the Passion. On the contrary, all my joy is in seeing this suffering Godman. Sometimes it seems that my soul enters into Christ's side and this is a source of great joy and delight. It is such a joyful experience to move into Christ's side that I cannot put words to it.

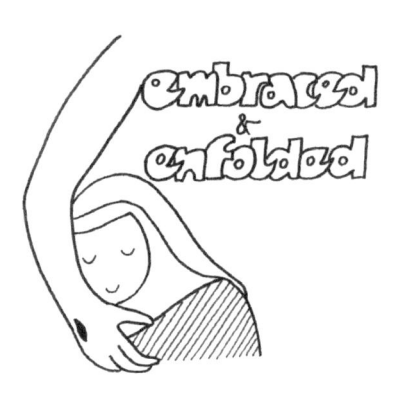

mary tell me...

The poverty of the Son of God

Once when I was meditating on the poverty of the Son of God I actually saw his great poverty within my heart. I saw too those for whom he made himself poor and I felt such sorrow and remorse that I almost fainted. I saw Jesus poor – poor in friends and relatives, poor and powerless to help himself. Seeing Jesus poor made me recognise my own pride in comparison and I could no longer feel joy.

Another time I saw how those who hated Christ hardened their hearts against him. He knew beforehand that they wanted to destroy him and he knew the hardships, pain and shame that would be his.

Then I cried out inwardly: 'O, holy Mary, mother of the afflicted one, tell me something of your son's pain that only you can recall. Surely you have seen more than any saint could tell me for you loved him more deeply than anyone.'

I realised then that neither the Blessed Virgin nor any other saint could find words to express the suffering of God's Son.

Another time I saw the great pain Christ felt in his soul, for he suffered out of his immense love for the human race. As we offend God in our soul, so I understood how Christ's soul felt such great pain at the way we commit numerous sins. I saw such deep pain in Christ's soul that my own soul felt the pain of it and all joy fled.

Angela with Christ in the sepulchre

On Holy Saturday I seemed to be with Christ in the sepulchre. I saw that he lay dead with his eyes closed. I kissed his breast then his mouth, from which emanated a fragrance impossible to describe. I placed my cheek on his, while he, with his hand, pressed me closely to himself. In my heart I heard him telling me, 'Before I was laid in the tomb I held you closely to me in this wise.' I did not see his lips move for he still lay as if dead. And my joy was immense and indescribable.

How poverty is the root of all virtues

God praised poverty as a great good because he chose it. If pride exists in us it is because we believe we possess something.

Humility is in us when we see that we are poor and possess nothing of our own. Poverty is the root of humility and of every good. Whoever is poor cannot fall into ruin or be deceived, for they would see how God loves true poverty.

Divine wisdom enables us to see our own defects and discover how truly poor we are in every way. Such a one loves God and does the works of love for God's sake. It was this wisdom that taught the Blessed Virgin. As she knew herself at the Incarnation, all doubts were removed and she entrusted herself to the Divine Goodness. Thus, knowing herself and knowing God's goodness, she was able to say, 'Behold the handmaid of the Lord. Let it be done to me according to your word.'

Christ too is bound in obedience to the Father. And when we understand this truth we can perform good works without any concern for merit.

Angela perceives God in darkness

Once my soul was lifted up, I saw the light and beauty and fullness that is in God in a way I had never seen before.

But I did not see love and I lost the love that was mine, being made non-love.

Afterwards I saw God in darkness. Darkness is what we perceive because God is so good that we can never understand him. Then my soul was granted a most certain faith, secure hope, and a continual security about God that took away all fear. I was made so sure of God that I could no longer doubt that I possessed him. It is this most efficacious good seen in darkness that is the cause of my sure hope, in which I am totally recollected and secure.

I find delight in the All Good, seeing nothing and everything at the same time. My hope lies in this secret good, a good most certain and hidden, which is accompanied by great darkness. All creation seems to overflow with God's presence, yet even this is inferior to the darkness which is the most secret good. It is the whole, whereas all else is but a part.

In darkness all feelings are also dark – no smile, no devotion, no fervour, no ardent love. The soul sees nothing and everything. All I have experienced and written about God is nothing compared to the stillness and beauty of this darkness.

When I have been in this state and it begins to fade, I see the God-man drawing my soul with great tenderness; sometimes saying to me, 'You are I and I am you.' Then I see his eyes and his face, so gracious and attractive as he leans to embrace me.

Angela chooses the bed that Christ was given by the Father

While I am in the God-man my soul is alive in the vision, even though I prefer the vision of God in darkness. Indeed I am in the God-man almost continually, and have been

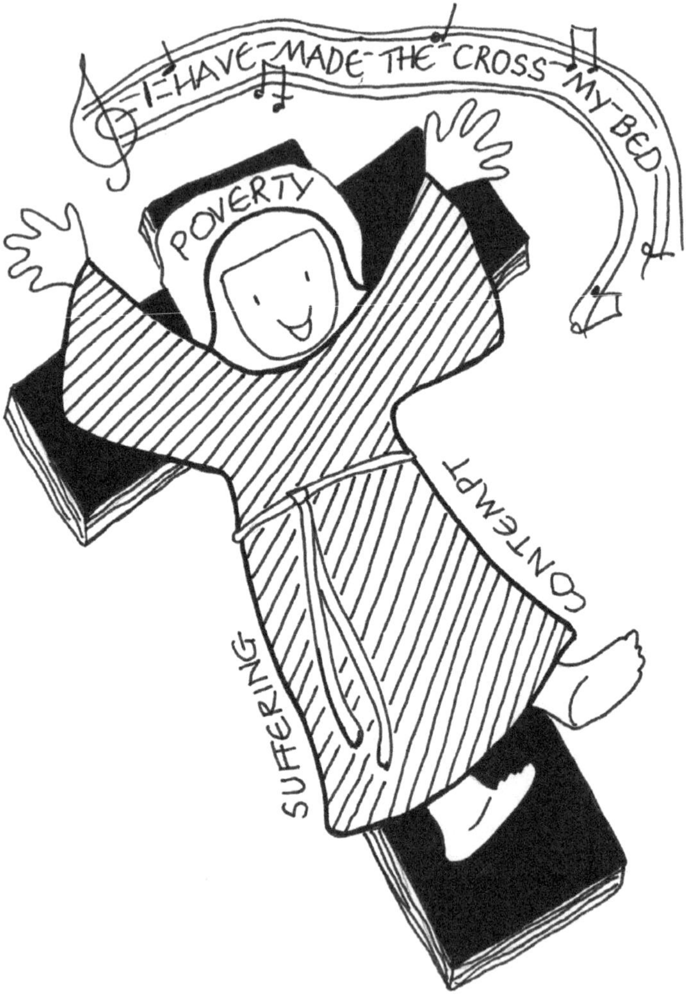
I HAVE MADE THE CROSS MY BED
POVERTY
CONTEMPT
SUFFERING

given assurance that there is no intermediary between Christ and myself.

Since that time there has not been a day or a night when I did not experience continual joy in Christ's humanity. My one desire is to sing and praise God in these words:

'I praise you God, my beloved:
I have made your cross my bed.
For a pillow or cushion,
I have found poverty,
and for other parts of the bed,
suffering and contempt to rest on.'

I rest on this bed because on it Christ was born, lived and died. God the Father loved this bed of poverty, suffering and contempt and gifted it to his Son; and the Son wanted to lie on this bed because he too loved it.

That is why Christ's bed is my bed. It is the bed of the cross, on which Christ suffered in body and even more in soul. On this bed I have placed myself and find my rest. On this bed I die, and through this bed I believe I am saved.

I just cannot describe the joy I feel when I remember the marks of the nails which pierced Christ's hands and feet on this bed. Humming, I say to the son of Blessed Mary:

'There are no words for what I feel.
What I see I never want to depart from
Because for me to live is to die.
Oh! Draw me then to yourself.'

Angela praises God's judgements

I like to recite a litany, praying to God as follows:

> *'Lord, deliver me by your coming.*
> *Deliver me by your nativity and your passion.'*

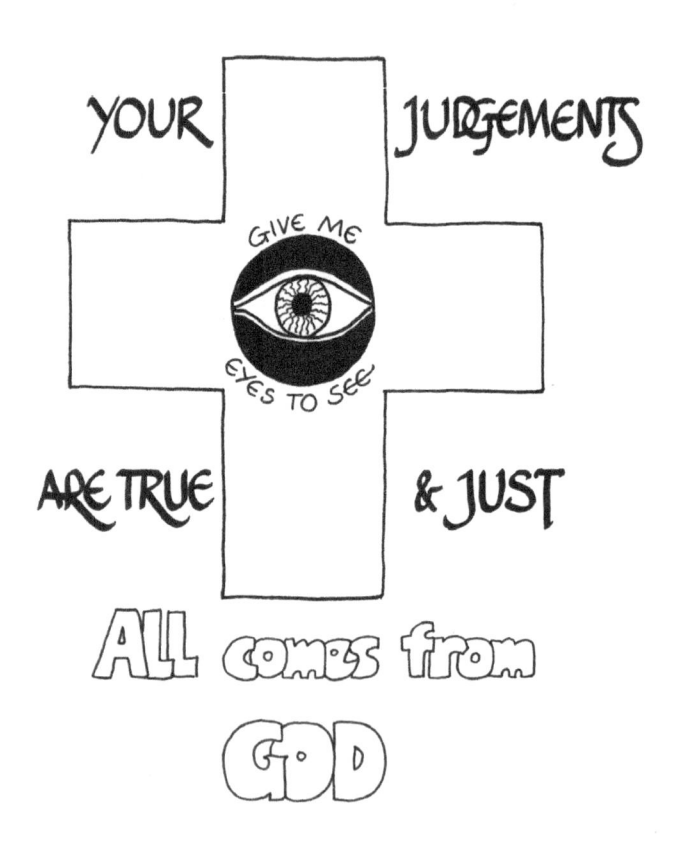

YOUR JUDGEMENTS ARE TRUE & JUST

GIVE ME EYES TO SEE

ALL comes from GOD

But nothing gives me greater delight than when I reach the invocation:

'Deliver me by your holy judgements.'

I proclaim these words with confidence because I do not recognise God's goodness more in one, or indeed many, holy people, than in one who is damned. My belief in the justice of God's judgements is unshakeable. They are so deep, and they all serve to benefit the good, for everyone who knows the depths of these judgements will benefit from everything that happens to them.

With Mary on the feast of Candlemas

On the feast of Blessed Mary of Candlemas (the Purification, February 2nd), while blessed candles were being distributed in memory of the Son of God being presented in the temple, my soul experienced its own presentation. I saw myself so noble and elevated that I cannot conceive how even the souls in heaven could have a greater nobility. And I realised that while my soul and the souls in paradise are endowed with nobility beyond our comprehension, how much less can we comprehend God the creator who is immense and infinite. I then presented myself before God with utmost confidence and without any fear.

This presentation was accompanied with a greater delight than I had ever experienced, with a new and excellent joy and with clear and new miracles.

After I returned to myself I discovered that I was glad to suffer any injury or pain for God's sake, as nothing could henceforth separate me from him. Furthermore, I delighted in the thought of my death. No one can imagine the delight I feel when I think of the day of my death.

FROM ANGELA'S 'INSTRUCTIONS' OR TEACHINGS

TEACHINGS ABOUT LOVE

Obtaining good love

Nothing is more strong and binding on the heart than love. But unless love is regulated we can fall into utter ruin. I am not speaking of evil love here, but of good, spiritual love.

It can happen that two or three people love each other intensely and want to be almost always together. But unless this kind of love is regulated, true love of neighbour either becomes carnal or is wasted in useless conversations and indiscretions.

When we are transformed in love we receive the necessary wisdom to regulate love of God and neighbour, so that love is expressed appropriately. When we are united to God we become less changeable; we acquire wisdom, maturity, depth, discernment, enlightenment and other virtues. Armed with these graces we cannot be deceived or fall into disorder. But if this wisdom is not yet ours we should not extend any special love to others.

We may act with the best of intentions and yet risk encountering the dangers of disordered love.

Binding oneself to another means that we must first have learned to live separately.

The properties of love

When we feel the heat of divine love we cry out and moan. It is as if a stone were flung into the forge to melt it into lime. It crackles when licked by flames, but afterwards, when baked, there is no sound.

Often in the beginning we seek divine consolations, but when these are withdrawn we cry out and complain to God, 'You are hurting me. Why?' An assurance of God's presence renders us tender so that we are satisfied with consolations and spiritual gifts. But when these are absent love grows and begins to seek the loved one. If we do not find him we pine for him. We no longer want consolations but only the beloved.

Once we are united to God we are placed in the seat of

my GOD & my All

truth, for truth is the seat of the soul. Then we no longer cry out, grow tender, or pine away. Wisdom and maturity make us see that we do not deserve gifts. We become ordered, strengthened, ready to face even death: and God expands our soul to receive all he wishes to give us. God becomes our All, and we seek only him. This enables us to accept God's will in everything and entrust ourselves to him with complete confidence.

The example of Christ

All his life the suffering God-man knew only the cross. His life began, continued and ended on the cross. It was a cross of poverty, pain, contempt and true obedience.

Since the father's heritage is handed on to his children, so those who love God should assume and claim this heritage too. The more perfect we are and the more we love God, the more we will strive to do what the suffering God-man does and avoid whatever is contrary to God's will. To love means doing everything to please the loved one.

On imperfect and suspect love

Many believe they are in a state of love when they are actually in a state of hatred. Many believe they possess God, when in actuality they love the world, the flesh and the devil. Some love God thinking he will protect them from physical ills. These people love their bodies and material things. They love their friends and relatives in a disorderly way, wanting to benefit from them and receive gifts from them. They love spiritual persons because they think they share a reflected holiness with them. Their natural gifts and talents are used to please others, not God. They love learning so that they can appear wise, and correct others so as to feel important.

Some love God imperfectly, wanting his gifts. They try not to offend God but only so as not to lose paradise. They love consolations and sweetness and they love God because they want to be loved in return. They love others with a spiritual love only because they think to gain honour and profit from associating with spiritual people.

It is so easy to go down wrong paths because we have an overly natural love for our friends and relatives and want to please them. In fact we find we cannot say 'no' when we should. So until we have attained the state of perfect love all other loves should be held in suspicion.

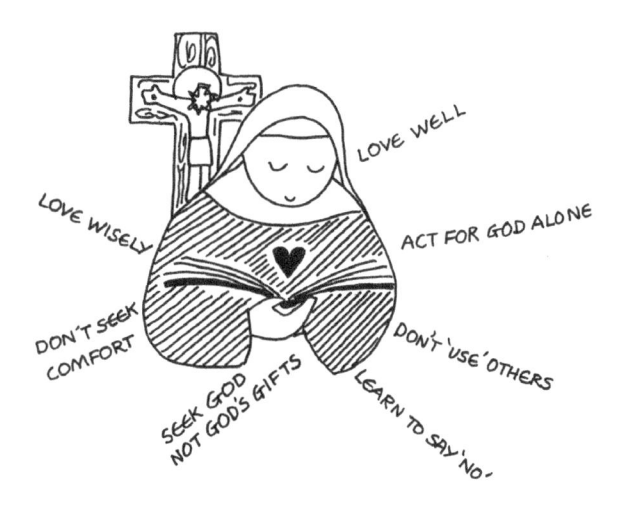

LOVE WISELY
LOVE WELL
ACT FOR GOD ALONE
DON'T SEEK COMFORT
SEEK GOD NOT GOD'S GIFTS
LEARN TO SAY 'NO'
DON'T 'USE' OTHERS

Perfect love

Perfect love is when we are drawn out of ourselves and into the vision of God. Then we understand that all has its being from the supreme Being, and we become wise, deep and mature. The vision of the supreme Being teaches us to love everything that comes from the supreme Being. Like the supreme Being we learn to stoop lovingly towards all creatures, rational and non-rational.

We can tell if we are in this state of love, true followers of the Son of God, in that the eyes of the soul are fixed upon him so that we love, serve and follow him, being gradually transformed into the divine likeness. The soul that loves does not live a life of self-indulgence but is willing to do penance and take up the cross. We do not consider that love dispenses us from the law; rather we make our own additional laws to keep us focused and walking the narrow path of penance and truth.

FIX YOUR EYES ON CHRIST
BE TRANSFORMED INTO HIM

The life of Christ was a life of penance, therefore we should never shrink from doing penance. Our love will then be constantly renewed and we will be set ablaze, ready to act with courage.

Those who do not live in the spirit of truth will make idols of the virtuous acts they perform. And their first idol will be the divine light given to them, for it is not their personal possession but God's gift alone.

Christ suffered for you

THE BOOK OF LIFE

God's ineffable plan

God's plan included the great sufferings of Christ. Christ saw beforehand, by means of divine light, all that he would have to suffer. This suffering was hidden from creatures but Christ knew it because he was completely united to God and was willing to do whatever the divine plan asked of him.

Christ also suffered because of his immense compassion towards us whom he loved in a heartfelt and visceral manner. He felt our sinfulness and took it upon himself. The deeper his love the deeper his suffering.

Christ also had compassion on himself, for he knew of his coming sufferings and had the sight of them constantly before him. He also felt compassion for his dear mother, for he loved her more than any other creature, having received his flesh from her own flesh. He knew that his sufferings caused his mother pain and he bore this suffering in himself, because of the divine plan.

Christ also suffered on account of his apostles and disciples, knowing they would suffer when his physical presence was gone.

And finally Christ suffered because of the sensitivity of his own soul. He knew the kind of knives, physical and spiritual, that his enemies would cruelly use against him; knives of cruel and evil hearts and tongues; knives of rage and evil intention. And he suffered from the sharpness of the nails – blunt, rusty and square, chosen because they would cause him the most extreme pain.

The meaning of Christ's suffering for our salvation

To show us something of the pain he suffered, Christ cried out, 'My God, my God, why have you forsaken me?' This cry was intended so that Christ's identity as God's Son would be revealed in his human suffering. He cried out to make known the acute and unspeakable sufferings he endured for us and he admonishes us to weep over them. As he said, 'My soul is sorrowful even unto death.' He suggests by these words that those who are his true followers should always weep over his sufferings.

However, by Christ's example of feeling abandoned he wants to give us hope and comfort in our own pain. Even if we may feel abandoned we should never despair for we can see that Christ ultimately profited from temptation and that he, being God, is ready to come quickly to our aid.

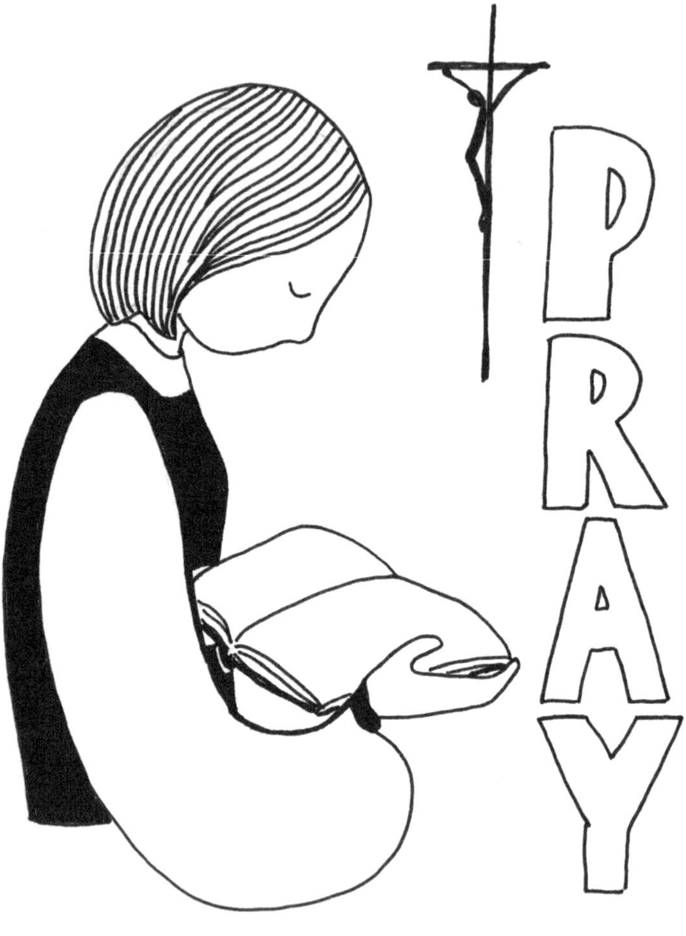
PRAY

ON PRAYER

The supreme necessity of prayer for our holiness

No one can be saved without the divine light. Divine light causes us to begin and make progress. It leads us to the summit of perfection, and if you have reached that sublime state and want to be ever more illumined and remain in the light, then PRAY.

If you want faith – pray.
If you want hope – pray.
If you want charity – pray.
If you want poverty – pray.
If you want obedience – pray.
If you want chastity – pray.
If you want humility – pray.
If you want meekness – pray.
If you want fortitude or any other virtue – pray.

And pray like this – always reading the Book of Life, that is, the life of the God-man, Jesus Christ, whose life consisted of poverty, pain, contempt and true obedience.

If you enter upon this path you will know temptation but if you want to overcome all difficulties – pray. True prayer turns evil into good and this is made possible by having a clean mind and body, with a right intention.

When we examine ourselves truthfully we can discern our hypocrisy and confess our neediness. Prayer enables us then to turn from self-preoccupation with a cleansed palate, ready to savour God's presence. It is through prayer that we obtain the powerful light to see God and ourselves as we really are.

Be on guard against false teachers of prayer

Know how to be separate before giving yourself to another person. Beware of flatterers and purveyors of revelations. Beware of those who only have the appearance of holiness. And beware of your own fervour. Follow it only insofar as it is conformed to the way taught by the Book of Life.

Be suspicious of those who say they are 'free' but whose lives are contrary to the life of Christ. God wanted his Son to be subject to the Law and he chose to be a slave and a servant. Those who follow him are ready to bind themselves by regulations that discipline them in daily life. Permissable things are thus sometimes not permissable to those who wish to live as Christ lived. And if you want to discern properly in this regard – then pray. The more you are tempted the more you should persevere in prayer.

Gold must be melted and purified and so must you. Persevere in prayer and you will be freed from temptation. Finally, through prayer you will be enlightened, freed, cleansed and united to God.

PURIFIED AS GOLD IN THE FURNACE

Effects of living a life of true prayer

The purpose of prayer is to enable us to know God and self.

This leads us to a state of true humility and with humility divine grace grows in the depths of the soul. We grow in humility as we read the book of the Life of Christ. But this only happens to the legitimate children of God who have devoted themselves to true prayer.

Those who have the spirit of true prayer will have the life of Jesus Christ, God and man, before them. In this Book of Life they will find all they could ever want. What is taught there does not puff anyone up. Therefore let this Book be read assiduously. Let the words penetrate deep within you and you will be taught all that you need to know. By reading it you will be able to accept suffering as being a consolation and a gift from God and you will be kept humble, in a state of divine grace.

Three kinds of prayer

There are three kinds of prayer: bodily, mental and supernatural. In the divine order we do not pass to mental prayer until we have first passed through bodily prayer. We do not attain supernatural prayer before we have passed through the prayer of the body and mental prayer.

The Hours of the Office should, as far as possible, be said at the proper time, with the mind in a state of quiet, and the body attentive and recollected.

JESUS
LORD SHOW ME YOUR FACE
in bodily, mental & supernatural prayer

The more you pray the more you will be enlightened.

The more you are enlightened the more deeply you will see God.

The more you see God the more you will love.

The more you see the more you will delight in what you see.

The more you understand the more you will be able to understand.

Afterwards you will come to the fullness of light because you will understand that you cannot understand.

The example of Jesus and Mary

The Son of God gave us an example of perseverance in prayer. He taught us how to pray by his words and deeds,

your will not mine

saying, 'Watch and pray, that you do not enter into temptation.' In other places in the gospels we see how he recommended this, how dear prayer was to him, and how, in his love for us, he said we should never neglect to pray. In the Garden his sweat became like drops of blood through the intensity of his prayer, asking for the chalice to be taken away if it were possible. This he asked on our behalf, preferring the divine will to his own, as should we.

The Blessed Virgin too is an example for us. She taught us to pray as she did when she promised God that she would remain a virgin. While she prayed, making this promise, divine light abounded in her ever more fully. She not only consecrated her virginity but her whole body and soul to God. In this light she understood herself and her God perfectly.

We pray differently from the Blessed Virgin, who had no need to seek mercy for her sins as we do. We pray to be enlightened and to grow in divine gifts, but God had purified the Blessed Virgin, chosen and adorned her uniquely. On earth she enjoyed something of what the saints enjoy in heaven. Their joy is the joy of incomprehension; that is, they understand that they cannot understand. It is this kind of comprehension that the Blessed Virgin enjoyed, for the full experience of our heavenly homeland could not be hers during her mortal life.

POVERTY

POWERLESSNESS

HANDMAIDEN — SERVICE

GOOD THIEF — TRUST

A MEDITATION ON POVERTY

Examples of perfect poverty

We have an example of true poverty in Jesus Christ, God and man. This God-man Jesus raised us up and redeemed us by poverty. His poverty was such that it concealed his power and nobility. He let himself be blasphemed, abused, scourged, crucified, behaving as one powerless to help himself. His poverty is a model for us to follow. Unlike him we do not have any power to hide, rather we must be aware of our great powerlessness.

Another example of true poverty is the glorious Virgin Mary. She taught us poverty in that she declared herself most lowly, just a 'handmaid', saying, 'Behold the handmaid of the Lord.' Acknowledgement of one's poverty is always acceptable to God.

We have another example of true poverty in the good thief who was crucifed with the God-man Jesus Christ. He had lived an evil life and done wicked things but once he received divine light and saw the goodness of God he immediately saw his own poverty, acknowledged it, and answered his companion who was insulting Christ, 'You are under the same condemnation as this man. Is there no fear of God in you? We are getting what we deserve, but this man has done no wrong.' Then he turned to Christ saying, 'Remember me, Lord, when you come into your kingdom.' And at that moment he was saved.

For us sinners to be aware of, and fully acknowledge, our poverty is the greatest satisfaction we can offer God and it makes us want to do penance without setting any limits.

The example of blessed Francis

Our blessed father Francis possessed ineffable light on poverty. He opened up a special way and showed it to us all. I cannot think of any saint who demonstrated, as Francis did, the way found in the Book of Life, whose model is Jesus Christ. Francis set his eyes on the path of poverty and never left it, and the effects were plainly seen in his bodily stigmata.

Because he set himself to follow this path with determination he was filled to overflowing with the highest wisdom, a wisdom which continues to fill the whole world.

Our blessed father Francis taught us two things: the first is to recollect ourselves in God so that the grace of the Holy Spirit can animate all we do. The Holy Spirit, having cleansed Francis in body and soul, made him truly holy and joined him to God in ineffable union. Being poor within and without, Francis was totally transformed. Not only did he make himself poor, but prescribed it for all, drawing his teaching from the Book of Life, that is, the life of the God-man, Jesus Christ. We can trust St Francis because he was no hypocrite, nor did he pray in vain.

Francis
TOTAL TRANSFORMATION
STRONG LOVE
STRONG DESIRE
SURRENDER TO
THE SPIRIT

The second lesson taught by blessed Francis was that of poverty, suffering, contempt and true obedience. Francis personified poverty within and without, and in this way he persevered to the end. He despised all that Jesus despised, loved all that Jesus loved. With great perfection he followed in the footsteps of Jesus so as to become conformed to him in all things.

If we love something intensely we want to possess it and the stronger we love the more strongly we desire. All that Jesus Christ loved, Francis, poorest of the poor, loved. He was continually being cleansed as his vision was purified. God gave him a unique vocation for the benefit of many others. Through prayer Francis came to plenitude and was uniquely gifted.

True freedom enables the Holy Spirit to teach us how to keep our souls and bodies in perfect order, recognising that we are sinners and do much that is wrong. Spiritual freedom is not about doing whatever we want and claiming that this is the way to grow in God.

The more perfectly we see, the more perfectly we love. Therefore the more we see of Jesus Christ, God and man, the more we are transformed into him by love. And the more we are transformed in love the more we will enter into the suffering we see in Jesus. Indeed, the more we love and see Christ's suffering, the more we will be transformed into his suffering through love.

GRACES RECEIVED IN ASSISI

A vision of the crucified Jesus

On the Sunday before the feast of the Portiuncula Indulgence (August 2nd), in the upper basilica of Assisi, during the elevation of the Host while the organ was playing the angelic hymn, 'Holy, holy, holy,' my soul was absorbed into the sovereign and uncreated God. While I was absorbed in this vision of God's fathomless depths the image of the crucified God-man appeared to me, looking as if he had just been taken down from the cross. His blood flowed fresh and crimson, as if the wounds were opened. The joints and tendons of the blessed body were distended due to the cruel stretching and pulling of his virginal limbs. The bones and sinews seemed torn out of their natural position, yet the skin was not broken.

As I looked I seemed to be totally transformed into the pain that Christ suffered on the cross. Those distended limbs made me feel pierced with sorrow, more so than I had been at the sight of his wounds. The body of the crucified Jesus stirred me to such compassion that the joints of my own body seemed to cry and lament. Through my compassion for the crucified Christ I was granted to contemplate fully his life and crucifixion.

Angela sees her Franciscan spiritual sons and daughters

While I was filled with joy and sorrow at the sight of Jesus I suddenly saw a multitude of my sons and daughters gathered around him. He embraced each one with great love and his hands drew each one's head to himself as he made them kiss the wound in his side. As a mother, my soul felt such deep love for my sons and daughters on the part of the blessed and crucified God-man, that it made me forget the inner pains I had felt at the sight of Christ's torments.

There seemed to be varying intensities in the way my sons and daughters were embraced and held to Christ's side.

Some he thrust deep into his side more than once, others he seemed to absorb deep into his body. The faces of some were completely covered with his red blood, others were red only on the lips. To each one he extended many blessings, saying, 'My children, show others the way of my cross, the way of poverty and contempt. I have chosen you for this.'

It is true that each of my sons and daughters received blessings in various intensities, but I did not reveal this to them. What matters is that everyone does their utmost to be conformed to the crucified Christ, and embrace his command to follow the way of the cross in contempt and poverty with all their strength.

I saw such deep and tender love for my sons and daughters shine in the blessed face of the God-man, as he pressed each one to the wound in his side, as well as blessing them with words. It is something impossible to express fully.

A grace at the church of the Portiuncula, St Mary of the Angels

On the day of the procession itself I went into the church of our Lady of the Angels and there I saw my sons and daughters being transformed by the divine majesty. It was reflected in my own face which shone with joy as I saw God's tender love being poured out upon my sons and daughters. I found endless satisfaction in just looking at them.

Then God made these demands of my sons and daughters, 'My beloved children, offer yourselves to me as a holocaust, a total sacrifice of body and soul.'

During the procession the image of the crucified God remained before my eyes – not in a carried image but given to me directly by God. And as Christ embraced my sons and daughters he said to them, 'I am the one who takes away the sins of the world. I have borne the burden of your sins and these will not be imputed to you in eternity. For this is the bath that cleanses you; this is the price of your redemption and your dwelling place. Do not be afraid to defend and show forth my way of life which is under attack. For I will always help and defend you.'

OFFERED AS A HOLOCAUST

all yours

The Blessed Virgin blesses Angela's spiritual sons and daughters

As we approached the church of the blessed Mother of God she, the queen of mercy and every grace, who had previously appeared so exalted and lifted up, now leaned down towards her sons and daughters and in a new and gracious manner redoubled her blessings. She kissed each one on the breast, some more, some less, and some she held closely in her arms as well as kissing them. Her love for them was so great that she seemed to absorb them into the almost infinite light within her breast. I did not see arms of flesh, but my sons and daughters seemed to be enclosed in a wonderful and very soft light. In this light the Mother of God hid them within her breast and held them with a great and deeply felt love.

St Francis speaks to Angela

During the first part of the Mass on the feast day of St Francis, he appeared to me and wished me peace. Then he praised the intentions of those sons and daughters who burned with zeal to observe the poverty prescribed by the Rule and exhorted them to grow in deeds as well as thoughts. He prayed that God's abundant blessings would fall on the heads of his children and mine. I was to tell them that they should have no fears, for he was with them and the eternal God would help them. He then blessed them so lovingly that he seemed to pour himself out totally in love for them.

FLOURISHING IN GOD'S GOODNESS

GOOD WORKS

PRAYER

KINDNESS

PENANCE

SERVICE

Peace

humility of **heart**
roots us in our nothingness

ON HUMILITY

A humble heart

Learn everything you need to know from the God-man, Jesus Christ. He gave himself as as example saying, 'Learn from me, for I am meek and humble of heart, and you shall find rest for your souls.' Note that Christ did not ask us to learn from him to fast, to despise the world, to live in poverty or perform miracles, although he certainly did all these things. But he simply said, 'Learn from me for I am meek and humble of heart.'

Humility and meekness are set forth by Christ as the firm foundation and basis of all other virtues. Virtue is only blessed when accompanied by a humble heart. Humility of heart is the matrix of everything, the root from which trunk and branches are nourished.

The Virgin Mary, forgetting all her other virtues, saw that the basic reason for the Incarnation was her humility, for she said, 'He has looked on the humility of his handmaiden.'

Who can find rest, peace and tranquillity of soul unless they are grounded in humility? The more we know ourselves to be nothing, the more we will praise the divine goodness, and from this root the other virtues will begin to blossom.

Love of God and neighbour spring from humility

Love of God and neighbour, the foundation of all virtue, has its roots in humility. For the more we see God lowering himself to our nothingness, the more we are set ablaze, transformed in love, and see God in every creature, recognizing in them the divine presence. So we find joy in our neighbour's good fortune, and are grieved at our neighbour's misfortune. Our disposition thus becomes kind with the kindness of God.

Seeing the sufferings of others we are not disposed to judge or despise the unfortunate. Rather, being enlightened by humility, we know we have not fallen because of the goodness of God, and not by reason of our own merits. In fact, on seeing the defects of others, God's transforming love makes us take those defects on ourselves. We feel the compassion of the apostle Paul who said, 'Who is weak that I am not affected by it?'

And as love takes its origin from the root of humility, the same can be said for faith, hope, and all the other virtues.

The characteristics of the humble

The life of those who are established in humility is very angelic, pure, kind and peaceful. And because humble people are kind, they are affable and loving. Kindness and meekness are the way to convert others. Nothing can trouble the peace of such persons.

Be kind, be humble, and quarrelling will cease. Do not keep trying to justify yourselves when criticised. Curb your tongue. Become in this way a true member of Christ's body.

How to acquire humility

Prayer is the way that leads to humility. In prayer we learn to look at and read the Book of Life, that is, the life, death and resurrection of the Crucified One. Looking at the cross gives us knowledge of our sinfulness: this leads to humility. And in the cross we see the outpouring of God's mercy upon us.

Gazing upon the cross we become aware of how we have sinned. So we weep for the Christ who died for us who are sinners. Looking at the Crucified One we begin to do penance for the many ways in which we have offended God. This is to become spiritually circumcised.

So examine your life carefully every day. If the time has been well spent, praise God. If not, grieve over the evil you have done. This is the true circumcision of the soul prefigured in Christ's physical circumcision.

TRUE LOVE

Three signs of true love

The first sign of true love is that the lover submits his or her will to the beloved. And this special and singular love works in three ways.

First: if the loved one is poor the lover strives to become poor, and if scorned the lover wishes to be scorned also.

Second: it makes the lover abandon all other friendships which could be contrary to this love. It is ready to leave father, mother, sister, brother, and all other affections contrary to the will of the beloved.

Thirdly: neither of the lovers can keep anything hidden from the other. In my opinion this is the highest sign which completes the rest. It is in the mutual revelation of secrets that hearts are opened and bound more perfectly to one another.

On becoming little

I want for you, my dear ones, what I want for my companion and for myself that you be united as one in mind and heart. I desire for you what leads from discord to unanimity, that is – becoming little. When you are little you do not consider yourself self-sufficient because of your knowledge or natural abilities. Rather, you are inclined to acknowledge your defects, striving to correct them.

To be little means not being a threat or a burden on anyone. Your words are not contentious even when others oppose you. For by following the way of littleness and poverty, disciplined zeal and compassion, you will be a clear mirror for those who wish to follow this way, even when your tongue is silent.

O beloved ones! I know my pride, yet I dare admonish you and lead you in the direction of humility. I long to hear that, having become little, you are united in heart and soul for without this unity I do not see how you can please God.

Become Little by unimportant

Tribulations lead to deeper conversion, growth, purification, trust in God & ultimately deeper tranquility

On tribulations

When you are afflicted and tested within and without it is a certain sign that you are loved by the beloved. Consider the sufferings of the Son of God who was afflicted, and this affliction was for our benefit.

There are three things which holy tribulations accomplish.

First: they make us turn to God, or if we have already done so they prompt a greater conversion and closeness to him.

Second: tribulations make the soul grow, for when rain falls on well prepared soil it germinates and bears fruit. In the same way tribulations make us grow in virtue.

Third: tribulations purify, comfort, and quiet the soul, giving it peace and tranquillity.

Do not try to change what is happening to you, for tribulations benefit not only yourself but others also.

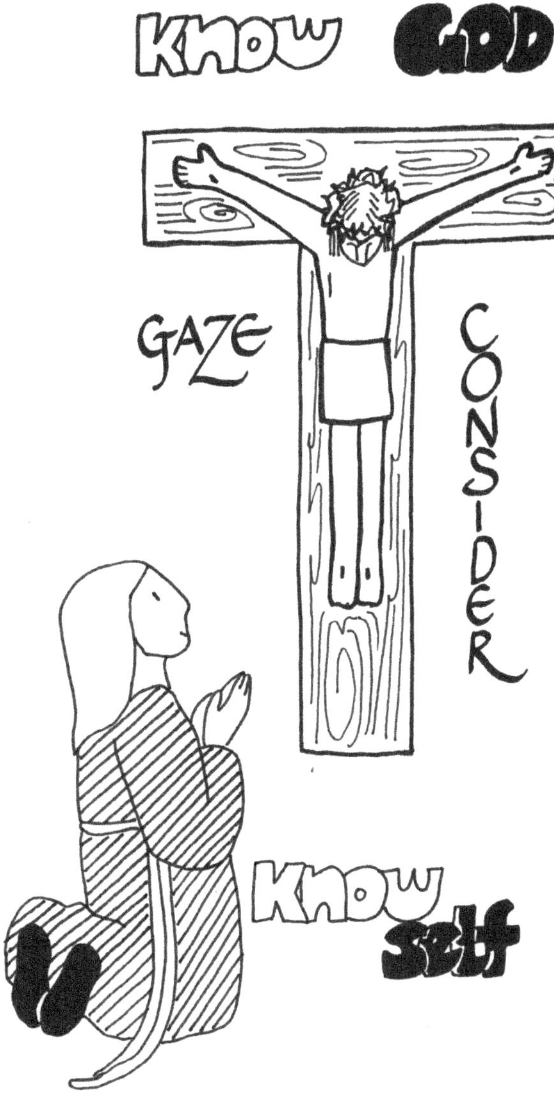
KNOW GOD
GAZE
CONSIDER
KNOW SELF

ON THE TRUE KNOWLEDGE OF GOD AND SELF

Coming to know oneself

Knowledge of God and knowledge of self are the only two things that I find pleasure in speaking about, apart from the admonition to remain continually in one's cell. I believe that anyone who does not know how to do this should not go anywhere else seeking other good things.

My dearest children, of what use are revelations, visions, feelings of God's presence, sweetnesses, spiritual gifts, unless we have a true knowledge of God and self?

Rid yourself of all negligence and laziness. Make sure that you pray, keep vigil, and perform good works whether you feel fervour or dryness. If necessary, force yourself to pray. This truly pleases God.

Never turn your eyes away from the suffering Godman. Keep your eyes fixed on him and your entire soul will be aflame. Review all his suffering and, whether or not you can practice contemplation, at least repeat vocal prayers attentively and frequently because what the lips say grants fervour and warmth to the heart.

TRANSFORMATION INTO CHRIST

Seven gifts which transform the soul into Christ Jesus

The more we grow in these seven gifts the more we become like Jesus.

The first gift is the love of poverty, by which we strip ourselves of the love of creatures and do not want to possess anything except our Lord Jesus Christ.

The second gift is the desire to be despised and villified and to want others to think of us in those terms, so that we live only in the heart of God.

The third gift is the desire to be afflicted and burdened with the many sufferings of body and heart which the most sweet Lord Jesus and his blessed Mother endured. Poverty, suffering and contempt conform us to Christ.

The fourth gift is to know we are unworthy to receive poverty, suffering and contempt. We must never presume we have become proficient in these gifts and every day we ought to make a new beginning in the hope of attaining them.

The fifth gift is to ponder continually on how poverty, suffering and contempt existed in Jesus Christ, and pray that he may send them deep into our hearts, so that we may be transformed and find joy in these things.

The sixth gift is to flee from anyone who gets in the way of our acquiring these gifts of poverty, suffering and contempt.

And the seventh gift is never to pass judgement on others but to place ourselves below everyone else.

We must want these gifts but not desire to feel them or want any accompanying consolation. Our one desire must be to become truly crucified with Christ.

Transformation through prayer

It is in prayer that we find God.

There are three types of prayer: bodily, mental and spiritual.

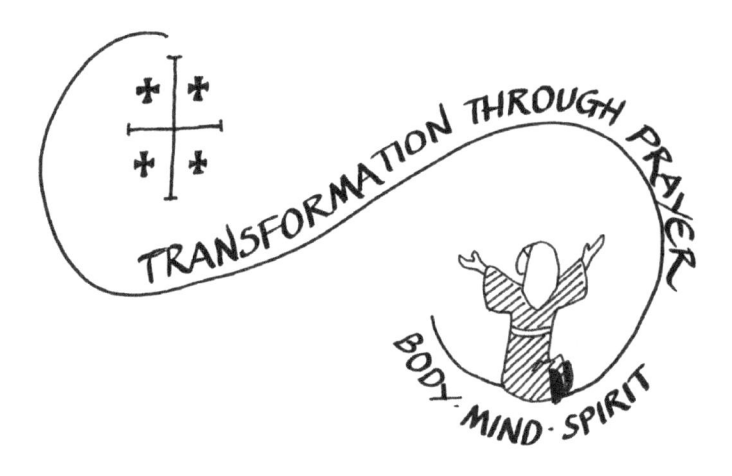

Bodily prayer takes place with spoken words and bodily movements such as genuflections. I never abandon this type of prayer which leads to mental prayer. Bodily prayer should be done with attention. Words should be said slowly and carefully, not run through as if trying to complete a certain number in a specific time, like little ladies doing piece work.

Prayer is mental when meditating on God occupies us completely, so that we can think of nothing but him. Mind and heart are filled with God without any distraction.

Prayer is supernatural when God gives this gift, filling us with the divine presence and stretching us beyond all our natural capacities. In this prayer we understand more about God than is possible when we are left to our own devices.

In these three schools of prayer we come to know who we are and who God is. When we know, we love. When we love we desire to possess the one we love. And this is the sign of true love: that the one who loves is totally transformed into the beloved.

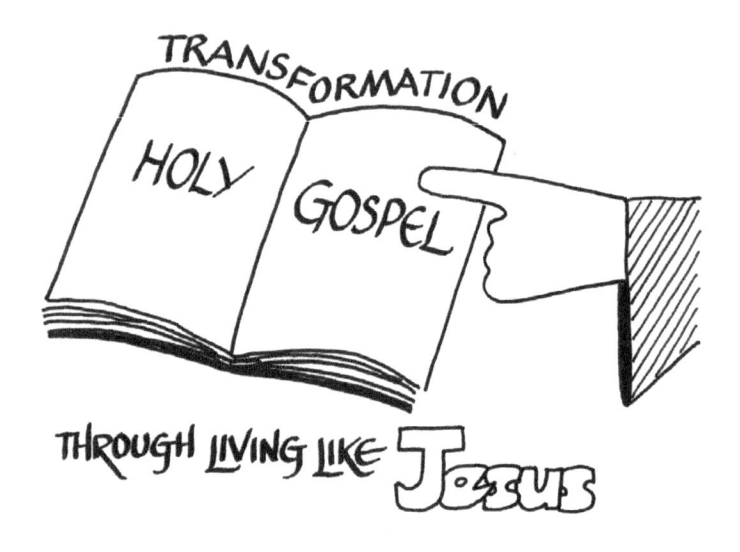

Transformation in Christ through the virtues

We should imitate Christ too in the virtues such as peace. We should be peaceful in words, in deeds and in our way of living. But we should be like lions in getting rid of our defects.

We should practice kindness and meekness, not just among ourselves but with everyone, not returning evil for evil but bearing everything patiently.

Let us be indulgent towards those who offend us by word or deed and respond calmly and kindly with a soul at rest.

Let us look at Christ and see how he bore offences with kindness. His example will give us strength not to hold a grudge.

Finally, we should imitate Christ so as to remain straightforward in word and deed, without deception or duplicity.

Carry him as he carries us

CONSOLING

STRENGTHENING

ABOUT THE EUCHARIST

Carrying Christ

Christ wants us to carry him within ourselves as he carries us – consoling and strengthening.

It is easier to see Christ as God incarnate, than to see him as uncreated God. However, we need to keep both these aspects in mind when we come to the Eucharist.

The Eucharist was manifested at the Last Supper, quite late and near night. It is linked to the long-lasting passion of Christ and the hardness of his death. It is a 'new mystery' which was foreshadowed in Holy Scripture. In it the bread and wine are transubstantiated into Christ.

Angels and saints both find new joy and sweetness in the Eucharist. So ponder this sublime mystery before Communion and approach the table with great respect, purity, fear and love.

Go to this mystery to be received.

Go pure in order to be purified.

Go fully alive in order to be enlivened.

Go as just in order to be justified.

Go united and conjoined to Christ in order to be incorporated, through him, with him and in him, God uncreated and God made man, who is given to us through the hands of the priest.

child of my heart

WHOEVER HAS NOT SEEN ME LITTLE WILL NOT SEE ME GREAT

PERSONAL GRACES FROM GOD

A vision on the feast of the Purification

On the morning of the feast of the Purification (February 2nd) I was in the church of the friars minor at Foligno when candles were being distributed and I heard God saying, 'This is the hour when Our Lady came into the temple with her son.' When I heard these words I felt such a great love welling up that it is impossible to say or understand anything about it.

Then I seemed to see Our Lady enter and I moved towards her with great reverence and fear. She reassured me and held her son out to me, saying, 'O lover of my son, receive him.' and she placed him in my arms. He seemed to have his eyes closed as though asleep and was wrapped in swaddling clothes. As if wearied from the journey, Our Lady sat down. Her gestures were so beautiful and gracious that it was exceedingly sweet to look at her and admire her. I turned again and again to look at Our Lady and then at her child. Then suddenly the child was left naked in my arms. He opened his eyes, raised them and looked at me. I saw and felt such an overwhelming love at his look that I pressed my face close to his as he lay in my arms. Such a fire emanated from the naked child's eyes that I was unspeakably moved and benefitted in my soul.

Then God appeared to me in majesty and said, 'Whoever

has not seen me little will not see me great.' And he added, 'I have come and offered myself to you; now it is your turn to offer.' In a marvellous and indescribable way I offered myself to him, and then I offered by name some of my sons and daughters, individually and together. I cannot describe the joy and delight I felt when I saw God accept this offering with such kindness.

'I HAVE NOT LOVED YOU IN JEST'

A grace during Holy Week

On the Wednesday of Holy Week I was meditating on the death of the Son of God incarnate and trying to empty my soul of everything else, so that I could be more recollected about his passion and death.

While I was engrossed in trying to do this, a divine word sounded in my soul which said, 'My love for you has not been in jest.' These words struck me like a mortal blow, for immediately the eyes of my soul were opened to the truth. I saw the love and all the acts and sufferings of the Son of God, all that he had endured in life and in death because of his inexpressible and visceral love for me and I understood in my heart that his love had not been in jest, while my love for him had been just playing games, never true. And at this I felt I could die of pain.

A vision of the church of the Portiuncula.

When I was about to enter the church of the Portiuncula so as to receive the Indulgence (on August 2nd), I was holding the hand of a certain woman who wished to help me. The moment I placed my foot over the threshold of the church I was suddenly enraptured and stood still. I seemed to see the church expanding by the power of God into a church of astonishing greatness and beauty. Everything about the church was totally indescribable. It was amazing how the church expanded as I set foot in it, for the church of St Mary of the Portiuncula is extremely small.

Christ and St Francis come to Angela in her illness

While I lay in bed very weak and afflicted in body, the God-man Jesus appeared and consoled me delightfully. He began by showing me the compassion that moves him and which is so pleasing to those who are sick. Then he said, 'I came here to serve you and I want to serve you.' He sat next to my bed and was so loving towards me that I cannot describe the joy and delight I felt.

I saw him more clearly with the eyes of my soul than of my body.

After this he showed me the blessed Francis saying, 'Here is the one who, after me, you have loved so much. I want him to serve you.' Then blessed Francis showed me the intimate love and kinship he felt for me, and it was great in every way. Afterwards he spoke secret words to me, finally saying 'You are my only true born child.'

'YOU ARE MY ONLY TRUE-BORN CHILD'

May God bless you all

'I LEAVE YOU MY INHERITANCE'

'LOVE ONE ANOTHER · SUFFER for OTHERS DO NOT JUDGE'

ANGELA'S DEATH

When Angela was near death, the very day before she died, she frequently said, 'Father, into your hands I commend my spirit and my soul.' That very day her sufferings ceased. Whereas before she had been tormented internally and externally, now her body lay in a state of great rest and happiness, as if the joy promised her was already effective. Several friars surrounded her and celebrated the Divine Office in her presence.

It was during the last hour of that day, the Octave of the feast of the Holy Innocents, that she died peacefully, as if falling asleep. Before this she had prayed for each of the sons and daughters God had committed to her care and for whom she had suffered and prayed.

The venerable spouse of Christ, Angela of Foligno, passed from the shipwreck of this world to the joys of heaven in the year of our Lord 1309 on January 4th.

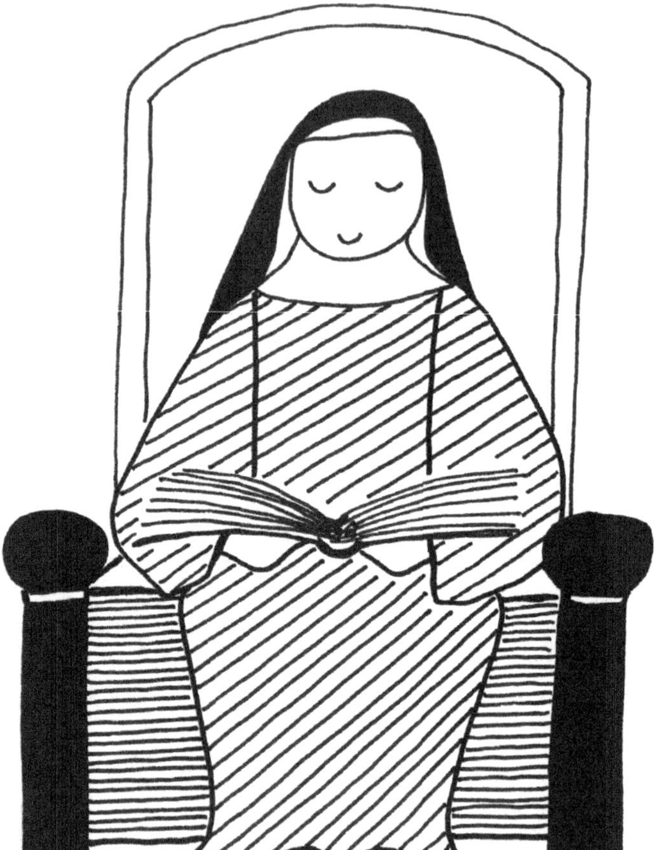

EPILOGUE

Let worldly wisdom, coming from proud teachers who talk big but do nothing much, be confounded by God's wisdom. God raised up a woman in the lay state, bound by worldly ties – a husband, children, wealth, possessions – unlearned and frail. But by means of the power infused into her by the cross of Christ she renewed the wisdom of gospel perfection. She showed the way of Jesus Christ that had become obliterated for we had been told by the mighty that it was a way impossible to follow. But Angela showed it was possible and even easy, leading as it did to the highest delight for the virtuous.

> O, heavenly wisdom of gospel perfection!
> You have shown up the foolishness of the wisdom of this world! Through Angela, you, O, God, have raised up against men a woman,
> against the proud someone humble,
> against the clever someone simple,
> against the educated someone unschooled,
> against religious hypocrisy someone who despised herself,
> against empty talkers and idle hands a marvellous zeal,
> against the prudence of the flesh the prudence of the Spirit which is the science of the cross of Christ.

Thus a strong woman brought into the light what was buried by blind men in their worldly speculations.

She is truly a shining light, a mirror without blemish, an image of God's goodness.

She makes all her sons and daughters prophets and friends of God.

She is a teacher peerless on earth.

Thanks be to God always. Amen.

FOR FURTHER READING

TEXTS

Angela of Foligno, The Complete Works, Translated and Introduced by **Paul Lachance OFM,** Classics of Western Spirituality Series, Paulist Press, 1993.

Angela of Foligno's Memorial, **Christine Mazzoni & John Grignano,** Library of Medieval Women, D.S. Brewer, 2000.

The Visions, Revelations and Teachings of Angela of Foligno, **Margaret Gallyon,** Alpha Press, 2000.

RELATED READING

Burr, David: *The Spiritual Franciscans,* Pennsylvania State University Press, 2001.

Heater, James & Colleen: *The Pilgrim's Italy,* Inner Travel Books, Nevada, 2003.

McGinn, Bernard: *The Flowering of Mysticism, Men & Women in the New Mysticism 1200-1350,* Independent Publishing Group, 1998.

Mc Namara, Jo Ann Kay: *Sisters in Arms,* Harvard University Press, 1996.

Obbard, Elizabeth: *Medieval Women Mystics,* New City Press, New York, 2007.

Underhill, Evelyn: *The Blessed Angela of Foligno* (reprint), Kessinger Publishing, 2010.